Tap It! Pat It!

Written by Emily Hibbs

Tap it.

Pat it.

Sit in it.

Tip it.

Dip it.

It is a pit.

Nip it!

Steam & Diesel Memories : 1950's – 1980's

No. 61: CAMBRIAN LINES

Photographs **Gavin Morrison**

Copyright Book Law Publications 2013

ISBN 978-1-907094-64-4

INTRODUCTION

The Cambrian Railway came about by the amalgamation of 5 railways

The Oswestry Ellesmere and Whitchurch Railway.

The Oswestry and Newtown Railway.

The Llanidoles and Newtown Railway.

The Newtown and Machynlleth Railway.

The Aberysthwyth and Welsh Coast Railway.

The Headquarters were established at Oswestry in a fine station building in July 1865. It still stands today and part of it is occupied by the Cambrian Heritage Railway Society. Due to the railways, the population of Oswestry rose from 5500 in 1861 to over 10000 forty years later. The main locomotive shed and works were at Oswestry. The shed closed in 1965 and the works in 1966.The Cambrian Railway covered 230 miles of track of which about 115 are still in use today. In 1911 the company had 91 locomotives and by the time the railway was taken over by the GWR in 1922, this had only risen to 94 plus 5 narrow gauge ones. By October 1867 all the Cambrian Lines were built.This book is intended to briefly cover the lines from the late 1950s to the late 1980, when services were taken over by Sprinter units. Due to weight restrictions, the lines were operated by smaller locomotives.From nationalisation these were mainly the Cambrian 0-6-0s, the ex GWR 4500 2-6-2Ts.the 4-4-0 Dukedogs, the Collett 0-6-0s and the Manor 7800 4-6-0s, followed by the standard BR 2MT,3MT and 4MTs After dieselisation ,the DMUs predominated on passenger workings.with Class 24 and 25s, and eventually class 37s. Class 20s occasionally appeared.The Cambrian Lines have always been a very much self contained system and today this is still the case. All the services are worked by Arriva Trains Wales class 158s, which are maintained at Machynlleth and fitted with the new ETRMS signalling equipment, as well as the 4 Network Rail class 97/3s.The book is intended to show the main locations and features along the lines. Owing to the relatively few trains, several pictures of the same train are included to give the coverage,as back in the 1960s and, even into the 1980s, it was easy to follow the trains, as they stopped frequently and the roads were quiet.   Gavin Morrison 2013

Cover picture: **Standard 4MT No 75033 bursts out of the cutting at Commins Coch on the climb from Machynlleth to Talerdigg summit on the last steam hauled up "Cambrian Coast Express."**
Date 4 March 1967. Gavin Morrison

Previous page: **The down "Snowdonian", 7.40am Euston-Pwllheli, crossing Barmouth Bridge headed by Class 37/4s Nos 37430 "Cwmbran" and 37427 "Bont Y Bermo".**   **Date 16 May 1987. Gavin Morrison**

Printed and bound by The Amadeus Press, Cleckheaton, West Yorkshire

First published in the United Kingdom by Book Law Publications, 382 Carlton Hill, Nottingham, NG4 1JA

(*above*) Oswestry was the headquarters of the Cambrian Railway with the station opening on 1 May1860 until closure on 7th November 1966. The Cambrian system extended to Whitchurch 8 miles beyond Oswestry, plus Wrexham and to Aberysthwyth [78 miles], Pwllhelli [132 miles] and Talyllyn Junction near Brecon, plus some branches. One of the 29 "Dukedogs", No 9012 is at Oswestry station ready to leave for Whitchurch. The old fashioned looks of the class suggest they were built much earlier than the actual building dates between 1930 and 1936. They were primarily designed for the ex Cambrian lines and gave excellent service for around 30 years, until replaced by the BR standard classes. The last ones were withdrawn in October 1960. Fortunately No 9017 survived into preservation and has been restored to working order. *Date 15th July 1952. Gavin Morrison.*

(*below*) The "Farewell to The Cambrian Tour", organised by the Midlands branch of the Stephenson Locomotive Society, has arrived at Oswestry station from Welshpool, before departing for Whitchurch and covering the Llanfyllyn branch. No 7802 "Bradley Manor" was the motive power, with Ivatt 2MT No 46512 for the branch. *Date 17th January 1965. Gavin Morrison.*

Passenger services were withdrawn on the Welshpool and Llanfair railway in 1931 but freight continued until 1956. The line was 2ft 6½in and was part of the Cambrian Railways, before being taken over by the Great Western in 1923. Two locomotives were built for the line by Bayer Peacock in 1902; No 822 "The Earl" withdrawn 1961 and No 823 "Countess" in 1963. After the line closed, they were stored in Oswestry works, where they are seen in this picture. The line became a heritage railway in 1963 and both locomotives have been returned to working order.

Date 21st June 1958. Gavin Morrison.

Standard 2MT 2-6-0 No 78006 at Llanfyllin station is ready to leave with the 1.25pm service to Oswestry. New in 1953, No 78006 was allocated to Oswestry shed [89A] and remained on the Cambrian lines until September 1962. It then moved to Gloucester until withdrawn in December 1965. Lanfyllin station opened in July 1863 and services lasted over 100 years, until complete closure of the branch came on 18th January 1965. *Date 5th March 1956. Hugh Ballantyne.*

The majority of the Great Western "Manor" class locomotives spent much of their careers working the Cambrian Lines. No 7802 "Bradley Manor" was no exception and it worked the "Cambrian Coast Express" frequently and was kept in immaculate condition by Aberysthwyth shed for the duty. It was transferred away to Tyesley in November 1962 and then to Shrewsbury in January 1965. It was selected by Shrewesbury shed to work the SLS "Cambrian Farewell Special", where it is shown climbing the 1 in 330 gradient at Arddleen, between Welshpool and Oswestry. It was withdrawn in October 1965 but passed into preservation and is now based on the Severn Valley Railway.

Date 17th January 1965. Gavin Morrison.

"The Cambrian Scenic Tour" was organised by the West Riding Branch of the Railway Correspondence and Travel Society. It started at Leeds and headed for Welshpool and Towyn giving the passengers the opportunity to travel on the narrow gauge Talyllyn and Welshpool and Llanfair railways. Class 40 D348 hauled the special throughout, much to the surprise of the passengers, as was believed that class 40s were banned over the bridge at Dovey Junction and Barmouth where the train reversed. The special arrived at Towyn without incident, although on the return, the crew apparently contacted control, pointing out they had a class 40 and was it in order to continue. Control took the view that, as they had arrived OK, it should be alright to return. It was probably the first and only time a heavy class 40 crossed the bridges on the Pwllheli line. The special is seen in the station at Welshpool on the outward journey.

Date 3rd May 1969. Gavin Morrison. 7

This picture is taken at Welshpool station and shows one of the famous GWR "Moguls" No 7336, ready to leave on the 3.20pm train to Shrewsbury. These fine locomotives were built over a period 22 years and could work over virtually all the GWR lines. They were designed by Churchward and the first example appeared in 1911. Ultimately 342 were built, Collett built 20 new ones in 1932 with minor modifications, which were easily identified by the side window cabs, illustrated here with No 7336. This batch were renumbered from 9300-21 to 7322-7341, 7336s previous number being 9314. No 7336 was allocated to Shrewsbury in January 1959 until withdrawn in August 1962. *Date 31st March 1962. Hugh Ballantyne.*

The down "Cambrian Coast Express" is taking water at Welshpool, while the driver takes a look around No 7823 "Hook Norton Manor". No 7823 was new in December 1950 and was allocated to several sheds before arriving at Machynlleth [89C] in March 1959. It stayed until November 1962 when it moved to Tyeseley. It was withdrawn in July 1964 after less than 14 years service. There was a turntable at the far end the yard as well as a water tower. Notice the British Road services office also in the yard.   *Date 31st March 1962. Hugh Ballantyne.*

There appear to be more enthusiasts than passengers to greet the arrival of the SO 10.10 Aberysthwyth-Wolverhampton, headed by Class 25s Nos 25259 and 25297. Welshpool station was opened on 14 August 1860 and this fine building was taken out of use as a station on 16 May 1992 to accommodate a road widening scheme, the present station now being to the left of this picture. The old station building is still in use as a small shopping centre. Class 25 No 25259 lasted until 21.8.1986 after 20 years of service and No 25297 was withdrawn on 3.12.1985 with 20 years on the books. *Date 15th September 1984. Gavin Morrison.*

The down "Cambrian Coast Express" is shown leaving Welshpool with Standard 4MT No 75021 piloting No 7823 "Hook Norton Manor" in the usual immaculate external condition, in which Aberysthwyth kept the locomotives allocated to the express. Standard No 75021 had only been transferred to Machynlleth the previous month but it was the beginning of the process of eliminating ex GWR from the Cambrian lines. Details of No 7823 have been given on page 10. No 75021 went new to the Western Region in November 1963 and moved around, until being allocated to Machynlleth in May 1962. It then moved to Croes Newydd in 1963 and then joined the London Midland region, lasting until January 1968.

Date 2nd June 1962. Gavin Morrison.

Thirty one class 37s were selected for refurbishment to class 37/4s, which included the fitting of electric train heating and they duly appeared in 1986. Six were allocated to Cardiff Canton, primarily to work the Cambrian line and the north and west services; the rest went to Scotland. Cardiff kept the locomotives [37426-37431] in excellent external condition, as can be seen in this picture of No 37427 piloting 37430 approaching Welshpool on the up "Snowdonian" 15.30 Pwllheli-Euston. Additional class 37s were drafted in on summer Saturdays to work the extra services, as will be illustrated later. All six of the Cardiff locomotives were allocated appropriate Welsh names; No 37427 receiving "Bont y Bermo" at Barmouth station on the 13th April 1986 and No 37430 "Cwmbran" at Cwmbran station on 11th May 1986. No 37427 was withdrawn in May 2006 and 37430 at the end of December 2007. *Date 16th May 1986. Gavin Morrison.*

Newtown is one of the main towns on the ex Cambrian lines situated 13 miles west of Welshpool. The original station opened in 1859 but was replaced in 1861. Here the up "Cambrian Coast Express", headed by one of Cardiff Cantons class 37/4s No 37429 'Eisteddfod Genedlaethol,' waits for the arrival of the 6.20 SO Birmingham-Aberysthwyth, headed by Buxton allocated class 37/5s. They were diagrammed for this train during the summer of 1988. Nos 37680 and 37682 were the locomotives on this date.

Date 18th June 1988 Gavin Morrison. 13

A 9 car DMU set arrives at Newtown on the 8.43 ex Birmingham to Barmouth, headed by an ex Inter city class 120. The class was introduced in 1957, with 130 powercars and 64 trailers, which were built at Swindon by 1960. Initially they were introduced on the Birmingham South Wales services. Gradually they were allocated to a wide variety of secondary services, with the final withdrawals taking place in October 1989. The picture is dominated by the Royal Welsh Warehouse built in 1895. *Date 1st September 1984. Gavin Morrison.*

A view from the west end of Newtown station of the class 120 DMU departing. Details on page 14.

Date 1st September 1984. Gavin Morrison.

Newtown had a population of around 10,000 at this date but there is little sign of any people waiting to catch the 'up' 'Cambrian Coast Express' as it enters the station headed by Standard MT 4-6-0 No 75048. It was new to Accrington shed in October 1953 and then went to Bank Hall at Liverpool until 1966. It moved to Cross Newydd for the last year of steam on the Cambrian lines and then continued in service till the end of steam in August 1968.

Date 11th February 1967 Gavin Morrison.

Two weeks before the end of class 25s working the summer Saturday extras on the Cambrian lines, Nos 25254 and 25298 depart Newtown on the 7.35 Euston-Aberysthwyth. No 25254 was new to Tinsley in March 1966 and put in just over 20 years service before being withdrawn. No 25298 also went new to Tinsley, in April 1966 and was withdrawn in March 1985. *Date 1st September 1984. Gavin Morrison.*

Moat Lane junction was near the village of Caersws and the first station was opened in 1859, by the Llanidoles and Newtown railway. On the opening of the line to Machynlleth in 1863, the station moved a short distance. Through services to Brecon commenced in 1864, the line becoming known as the Mid-Wales line, travelling through very sparsely populated countryside. In spite of this, the services continued until 31 December 1962. This picture shows plenty of activity at the station. On the far left is Ivatt 2MT 2-6-0 No 46521, with No 46523 in the bay platform. The rear of the 2.30pm Aberysthwyth-Oswestry is alongside and to the right is BR Standard 2MT No 78002 on the 4.20pm Newtown to Machynlleth. The station had 5 platforms and a two road shed. The station buildings were demolished shortly after closure. *Date 7th June 1960. Hugh Ballantyne.*

(*above*) The town of Rhayader has a population of just over 2,000 and is in the centre of Powys. The station, opened in 1864, was in the village of Cwmdauddwr on the opposite side of the river Wye and remained open until the line closed on 31 December 1962. The nearest station is now at Llandrindod Wells 12 miles away. The station site was cleared and is now used by Powys Council Highways department. Ivatt 2-6-0 No 46524 is at the station with an afternoon train to Brecon. No 46524 went new in April 1953 to Oswestry and remained allocated to the Cambrian shed, until withdrawal in February 1965.

Date 2nd June 1962. Gavin Morrison.

(*below*) The crew invited myself and a friend onto the footplate for a ride south to Three Cocks Junction. This view was taken as No 46524 approached Builth Road, which was the connection station for the Central Wales Line on the high level platforms [it is still open] The London North Western line to Swansea [Central Wales Line], opened in November 1866 and the station was named Builth Road, as it still is today. *Date 2nd June 1962. Gavin Morrison.*

Three Cocks Junction is where the Mid Wales Line joined the ex Hereford Hey and Brecon Line, which was taken over by the Midland. The name Three Cocks Junction came from a local Inn and the present site took its name from the station, which is now a garden centre. It was another remote junction that the Great Western inherited from the Cambrian Railway, as the only town near was Hay-on-Wye 8 miles away. The line continued to Brecon, passing Talyllyn Junction en route. Services on both lines ended on 31 December 1962. Ivatt 2-6-0 No 46518 has just arrived from Moat Lane in the pouring rain and is connecting with a train to Hereford.

Date 11th September 1962. Gavin Morrison.

Talyllyn Junction station was in a delightful settting and was a short distance from Brecon. It was where the Cambrian line ended and where it joined the Brecon and Merthyr, which travelled over the steeply graded route via Torpantu and Pant to Merthyr. Great Western Collett 0-6-0 No 3201 is waiting with a train to Newport, to make a connection with a service from the Mid Wales line. No 3201 was allocated to Newport Ebbw Junction [86A] at the time but transferred to to Templecombe on the ex Somerset and Dorset Joint Railway, before withdrawal in May 1965.

Date 10th September 1962. Gavin Morrison

The 10.10am SO Euston-Aberysthwyth is ready to leave Caersws running 3½ hours late, after the failure of another pair of class 25s the other side of Welshpool. Nos 25285 and 25286 are the locomotives shown, both entering service at Tinsley in April 1984. No 25285 was withdrawn in September 1986 and 25286 in December 1985. Caersws is about a mile from the site of Moat Lane station and is the point where the line starts the 8 mile climb to the summit at Talerdigg. The station opened on 5 January 1863 and is still open.

Date 1st September. 1984. Gavin Morrison.

To mark the end of the regular use of Class 25s, on the summer Saturday extras on the Cambrian, the 14.00 from Aberysthwyth to Euston carried an unofficial headboard. The train is passing Pontdolgoch heading for Newtown with Nos 25034 and 25058. The station opened here on 5 January 1863 but was closed on the 14 June 1965, as it was less than 2 miles from Caersws. No 25034 was new to Toton depot in May 1963 as No D5184 and received the unofficial name of Castell Aberysthwyth/Aberysthwyth Castle in 1985. It was withdrawn on 22 December 1986. No 25058 also went new to Toton in February 1963 and was unofficially named Castell Criccieth/Criccieth Castle in 1985. Withdrawal came on the 3 February 1987. *Date 15th September 1984. Gavin Morrison.*

Two of Cardiff Cantons immaculate class 37/4s Nos 37427 'Sir Dyfed/County of Dyfed and No 37430 'Cumbran' descending the bank from Talerdigg summit at Carno on the 'Snowdonian' SO 15.30 Pwllheli to Euston. Being close to Caersws, the station closed on 14 June 1965, having opened on 5th January 1863, the same day as Pontdolgoch. [The locomotive details are on page 1].

Date 16th May 1987. Gavin Morrison.

No 7800 "Torquay Manor" was the first of the Collett light mixed traffic 4-6-0s, which were introduced in 1938. No 7800 spent the post nationalisation years allocated to the Wolverhampton Division [84] until August 1958, when it was allocated to Oswestry. It remained there until withdrawn in July 1964, only 2 months after this picture was taken. It looks in poor external condition but was going well with this heavy 9 coach "Gainsborough Model Railway Society" special near the summit at Talerddig, with no exhaust showing on a very hot day. The Society ran a special trip each year and this one was heading for Aberysthwyth for the passengers to have a ride on the Vale of Rheidol narrow gauge line. Six, [Nos 7808/7812/7819/7820/7822 and 7827] out of the class of 30 have been preserved.

Date 30th May 1964. Gavin Morrison. 25

On the last day of the "Cambrian Coast Express" as a named train and steam worked, Standard 4MT No 75033 blasts through the cutting at Talerdigg Summit for the last time. The locomotive had been cleaned by enthusiasts during the night and presented a fine sight with the headboard. As a named train, the "Cambrian Coast Express" first ran on the 15th July 1927 until 9th September 1939. It was reintroduced on 7th July 1951 until 4th March 1967. At the time of its construction, Talerdigg cutting, which was blasted through solid rock, was the deepest cutting in the world at 120 feet when it was completed in 1862. There was a little used station opened sometime between 1896 and 1901, which was closed in 1965.

Date 4th March 1967. Gavin Morrison.

"The Cambrian 125" special, headed by class 31 Dutch liveried No 31146 'Brush Veteran' is approaching Talerdigg summit, on the 1 in 56 gradient, with a set of smart Inter-City coaches. The class was not normally associated with the Cambrian lines but they were used for a brief period in the early 1990s. No 31146 entered service in November 1959 as D5564, receiving its name at Bescot depot on 27th August 1992. After suffering a main generator fire, it was stored in December 1998 and was at Booth Roe for scrap in July 2002.

Date 10th October 1992. Gavin Morrison.

There are 14 miles of continuous climbing from just east of Machynlleth to Taleredigg Summit, with just ½ a mile of level track through Llanbrynmair, when the gradient changes to 1 in 52 and then 1 in 56 to the summit 3½ miles away. Here, No 7803 "Barcote Manor" approaches the station in the usual immaculate condition for the locomotive, allocated to The 'Cambrian Coast Express' diagram from Aberysthwyth. The Pwllheli portion coaches are at the front of the train with Aberysthwyth ones at the rear. No 7803 "Barcote Manor" was built at Swindon in 1938 and was allocated to the Cambrian sheds in the post war years, until withdrawn in March 1965. There used to be a runaway siding here in case unfitted trains got out of control descending from Talerdigg. *Date 30th May 1964. Gavin Morrison.*

Standard 4MT No 75033 blasts its way up the 1 in 52 gradient for the last time with the Up 'Cambrian Coast Express', past Llanbrymair on its way to Talerdigg summit.[Details for No 75033 are on page 33]. *Date 4th March 1967. Gavin Morrison.*

The summer SO 10.10 Aberysthwyth-Euston was diagrammed for a pair of Buxton Railfreight Class 37/5s in 1988. Nos 37683 and 37682 are heading the train past Commins Coch, on the climb from Machynlleth to Llanbrymair and Talerdigg. The A470 main road crosses the railway here, where a halt was opened on the 19th October 1931 but closed on the 14th June 1965. No 37683 was new to Llandore depot as D6887, becoming 37187 under Tops and 37682 also went new to Llandore numbered D6936, changing to 37236 under Tops in 1974. Both locomotives are now owned by Direct Rail Services.   *Date 21st May 1988. Gavin Morrison.*

Cemmaes Road is 6 miles east of Machynlleth on a 1 in 163 gradient in the up direction. An immaculate class 37/4 No 37428 , 'David Lloyd George', passes on the 8.00 Pwllheli-Euston. The stationed opened in January 1863 and closed on 14th June 1965. There was a passing loop here [see page 32] but, judging by the piles of sleepers and the track, it had recently been removed. No 37428 entered service in May 1965 at Newport Ebbw [86A] as No D6981 and then No 37281 under Tops. It was converted to a class 37/4 in 1986 and eventually selected and repainted into the 'Royal Scotsman' livery, until relieved of these duties in 2001. It was eventually purchased by Harry Needle but not restored to working order and was awaiting cutting-up in January 2013.

Date 16th May 1987. Gavin Morrison. 31

The last named "Cambrian Coast Express" and the last day of regular steam on the Cambrian lines sees No 75033 [see details pages 33] passing through Cemmaes Road, when the loop was still in use. [Details of Cemmes Road Page 34].

Date 4th March 1967. Gavin Morrison.

Another view of the last "Cambrian Coast Express" between Machynlleth and Cemmaes Road, where the railway runs close to the River Dovey, which frequently causes severe flooding in the area. No 75033 was new to Bletchley in July 1953 before being transferred to the Chester area (6) in February 1955, moving 14 times within the Chester area and 5 times outside it before withdrawal in December 1966.

Date 4th March 1967. Gavin Morrison. 33

The last week-end of regular class 25s on the summer Saturdays extras on the Cambrian services, sees Nos 25034 and 25058 [loco details on page 23] passing the signal, which used to control the passing loop at Cemmes Road on the 14.00 Aberysthwyth-Shrerwsbury. Note the headboard.

Date 15th September 1984. Gavin Morrison.

(*above*) Machynlleth is a small market town with a population of just over 2,000 at the head of the Dovey [Dyfi] estuary in Powys and is prone to suffer from flooding in the immediate surrounding area. It is the most important centre on the ex Cambrian main line with a locomotive shed [codes 89C, 6F from 1963] until closure in 1966. Back in 1950 it has an allocation of 53 locomotives, which included those outbased at Aberysthwyth. This had reduced to 47 by 1959 and 13 in 1965. Seen at the west end of the main shed are 'Dukedog' No 9021. 4500 class 2-6-2T No 4549 and BR Standard 2MT No 78002. *Date 21st June 1958. Gavin Morrison.*

(*below*) The Cambrian class 89 0-6-0s were built between 1903 and 1919 and later became class 15 under the GWR. They were constructed by Bayer Peacock and Robert Stephenson and numbered 844 to 896 and were reboilered at Swindon by the GWR from 1924. The first to be withdrawn was No 888 in 1922, with the class becoming extinct in October 1954. No 864 is at Machynlleth shed one month after being withdrawn. None was preserved. *Date 17th November 1952. Hugh Ballantyne.*

No 4560 was built in 1924. The 4500 class was introduced in 1906 and totalled 175. No. 4560 spent the post 2nd war years allocated to the Cambrian area and is on Machynlleth shed [89C] in front of a stored Collett 2200 class 0-6-0. It was withdrawn 4 months after this picture was taken.

Date 28th March 1959. Gavin Morrison.

Aberysthwyth shed, around this period, kept one of the Manors in the 89 division in immaculate condition for working the 'Cambrian Coast Express' and Machynlleth usually had a very clean Collett 0-6-0 2200 class or 4500 2-6-2T to work the Pwllheli portion of the train. No 2255, a Cambrian locomotive since nationalisation, was the selected engine at this time, seen here on the shed looking very smart in the BR lined green livery. It was eventually withdrawn on the 21st April 1962. *Date 28th March 1959. Gavin Morrison.*

Looking west from Machynlleth station footbridge, class 25s Nos 25298 and 25254 are seen arriving with the 14.00 SO Aberysthwyth-Shrewsbury. No 25298 entered service at Tinsley in April 1966 numbered D7648, being withdrawn in March 1985. No 25254 also went new to Tinsley in March 1966 as D7604 and survived until April 1986.

Date 1st September 1984. Gavin Morrison.

This is a busy scene at the east end of Machynlleth, with class 37/4s Nos 37429 'Sir Dyfed/County of Dyfed' and No 37427 'Bont-y-Bermo', arriving with the 9.40am Euston-Aberysthwyth. Class 150/1 No 150118 sprinter waits in the loop to form the connection to Pwllhelli and is in the original Regional Railways livery. In the background is the site of the old steam shed, which has been converted into a DMU servicing depot and is still in use today. [Details of the class 37/4s are on page 24]. *Date 21st May 1988. Gavin Morrison.*

Dovey Junction, 3½ miles to the west of Machynlleth opened on the 14th August 1867. It is a remote location alongside the Dove Estuary and is the point where the Aberysthwyth and Pwllheli lines split. In this busy scene, No 7818 'Granville Manor' has arrived with the up "Cambrian Coast Express" from Aberysthwyth and 4300 class 2-6-0 No 6392, with a connecting service from Pwllheli. A Collect 2200 class can also be seen. No 7818 was not allocated to the Cambrian Division after WW2 until January 1960 and remained until withdrawn September 1961. No 6392 spent over 8 years at Machynlleth between 1954 and 1962, before being transferred and withdrawn in October 1961. Dovey Junction is still open.

Date 9th June 1960. Hugh Ballantyne.

Class 25s Nos 25254 and 25298 are powering away from Dovey Junction with the SO 7.25 Euston-Aberysthwyth, having made a connection with a Pwllheli train. [Locomotive details are on page 38]. *Date 1st September 1984. Gavin Morrison.*

Two 3 car class 120 DMUs leave Dovey Junction and cross the Dovey estuary working the 12.35 from Machynlleth to Pwllheli.

Date 1st September 1984. Gavin Morrison.

(*above*) The up SO 8.00 Pwllheli-Euston headed by class 37/4 No 37428 'David Lloyd George', runs along the coastline at Penhelig towards Dovey Junction near Aberdovey, [details for 37428 on page 34].
Date 16th May 1987. Gavin Morrison.

(*below*) Another view at Penhelig, this time showing the "*Cambrian 125 Special*" headed by class 31 No 31146 "Brush Veteran". [locomotive details on page 33].
Date 10th October 1992. Gavin Morrison.

Complete with headboard, class 4500 2-6-2T No 5541 heads the up Pwllheli portion of the "Cambrian Coast Express" along the estuary at Penhelig. Looking across the estuary at this point, the Aberysthwyth portion of the train would probably be in view. No 5541 was allocated to Machynlleth from the end of WW2 until January 1960, before moving to the 83 division and withdrawal in June 1962.

Date 28th. March 1959. Gavin Morrison.

At the end of the Dovey estuary, where the line heads north at Trefri near Aberdovey, Class 37/0s Nos 37298 and 37158 pass along the sea wall with the SO 7.30 Euston-Pwllheli. No 37298 went new as D6998 to Newport Ebbw in August 1965. It was sent to France in August 1999, returning one year later and then to Springs Branch for component recovery. No 37158 was new to Llandore in August 1963 and was taken out of traffic in August 1999, ending up at West Coast Railways at Carnforth, before being scrapped in 2008.

Date 21st May 1988. Gavin Morrison. 45

(*above*) After the London Midland took over the Cambrian lines. the ex Great Western locomotives were replaced mainly with BR standards. 4MT No 76040 pauses at Aberdovey station with the up "Cambrian Coast Express". According to records, it had just been transferred to Birkenhead so must have been on loan. The first Aberdovey station opened in October 1863 but was replaced by August 1867 and is still open today. No 76040 was withdrawn in March 1967 after just less than 12 years of service.   *Date 13st.August 1966. Gavin Morrison.*

(*below*) Due to flooding near Dovey Junction, this service from Pwllheli terminated at Aberdovey. The locomotive then ran round the stock, pushed the carriages out of the platform and is coming back into the down side. The standard 2-6-2T is green liveried No 82003. It entered service in May 1952 and was withdrawn in December 1966.   *Date 19th December 1964. Gavin Morrison.*

After taking the picture on page 45, the 7. 30 SO Euston-Pwllhehi stopped long enough in Aberdovey station for this picture to be taken, at the north end of it passing the golf course heading for Towyn. [Locomotive details on page 45].   *Date 21st May.1988. Gavin Morrison.*

The "Cambrian 125 Special," headed by class 31 No 31146 in Dutch livery, [details page 27] is leaving the popular seaside resort of Tywyn [Towyn]. The terminus of the Talyllyn Railway is just to the right of the picture. Tywyn stationed opened on the 24th October 1863.

Date 10th October 1992. Gavin Morrison.

In 1980 the bridge across the estuary of the Afon Mawddach at Barmouth was declared unsafe for locomotives, due to the wooden structure being attacked by Teredo worms. This ended freight operations north of Tywyn to Barmouth. Those that existed from the ammunitions factory at Penrhyndeudraeth were diverted via Maentwrog Road and the Conwy Valley line. This ban resulted in the extraodinary sight of class 128 Single Parcels Car units [built 1960] being used on ballast and permanent way workings, Here unit No 55995 waits alongside the signal box at Tywyn with two ballast wagons.   *Date 2ndApril 1984. Gavin Morrison.*

A JCB is loading the ballast wagons at Tywyn, before class 128 No 55995 hauls them north.

Date 2nd April 1984. Gavin Morrison.

Collett 0-6-0 No 2286 is leaving Tywyn with a stopping train from Barmouth to Machynlleth. Post WW2 it was allocated to the Cambrian sheds from July 1953 to August 1962, eventually being withdrawn in September 1964. At this date there was a fair amount of freight traffic generated at the station, judging by the number of wagons in the sidings. *Date 28th March 1959. Gavin Morrison.*

On a hot day in May, the driver leans out of the cab of class 37/4 No 37429 'Sir Dyfed/County of Dyfed' to get some fresh air, as it leaves Tywyn on the SO 8.00 Pwllheli-Euston. [Locomotive details on pages 53]. *Date 21st May 1988. Gavin Morrison.*

The section between Barmouth and Tywyn is probably the most spectacular on the Cambrian line as it follows the coast. Part of it is prone to rock falls and this avalanche shelter was built at Friog to try and avoid rocks falling onto the track. In the days of the annual steam hauled special from London to the Talyllyn railway, Manor class 4-6-0 No 7801 "Anthony Manor" and 4300 class 2-6-0 No 7314, head the special out of the avalanche shelter en route to Tywyn. They had taken over the train at Ruabon from King class No 6000 "King George V". Both locomotives were at Oswestry at the time, No 7801 being allocated to the 89 Division from August 1958 until withdrawn in June 1965. No 7314 was sent to Oswestry in September 1961 and lasted till February 1963. *Date 29th September 1962. David Mitchell.*

On a perfectly clear summer's day, the passengers on the SO 8.00am Pwllheli-Euston could look across Cardigan Bay to Pwllheli and the mountains beyond, as the train passes along the coast near Friog. No 37429 was new as D6600 to Newport Ebbw in August 1965. It became No 37300 in November 1973 and No 37429 on 13th March 1986 after conversion to a Class 37/4. It then carried two names "Sir Dyfed/County of Dyfed" which it received at Cardiff Canton on 2nd April 1987 and were changed to "Eisteddfed Genedlasthol" at Porthmadog Station on 5th August 1987. It was scrapped Febraury 2008 by EMR Kingsbury.   *Date 21st May 1988. Gavin Morrison.*

An early departure from West Yorkshire was necessary, to be in position outside Fairbourne, to photograph the SO 8.00 Pwllheli-Euston. Class 37/4 No 37429 [details on page 53] makes a fine sight with a set of Intercity liveried coaches, as it climbs away from Fairbourne. The station opened on the 1st July 1897 and is still open. *Date 21st May 1988. Gavin Morrison.*

A Pressed Steel Co 3 car Class 117 DMU is crossing the wooden single track bridge across the Afon Mawddach estuary at Barmouth. Opened in 1867 and built by the Aberysthwyth Welsh Coast Railway, it needed rebuilding in 1901. By 1980 it was discovered to be suffering from the ravages of the Terdo worm, which eats away at timber. This resulted in locomotives being banned from crossing it. It was repaired and locomotives allowed to use it again by 1985 but this was short lived. Further repair work was carried out and in 2005 locomotives were reintroduced. *Date 16th May 1987. Gavin Morrison.*

The class 117 dmu, seen in the previous picture, is seen leaving Barmouth with a summer extra working to Dovey Junction.

Date 16th May 1987. Gavin Morrison.

A good turnout of the local children greet the Royal Train, when it visited Barmouth, headed by two immaculate 4-6-0 Manors Nos 7819 "Hinton Manor" and No 7822 "Foxcote Manor." Both locomotives are now preserved. No 7819 is currently at the designer outlet village at Swindon and No 7822 at the Llangollen Railway.   *Date believed to be 10th August 1963. Railphotoprints.co.uk The late R A Whitfield.*

The mountains of Snowdonia can be seen in the background, as the SO 15.30 Pwllheli-Euston enters Harlech station. The train was named the 'Snowdonian' in the timetable but did not appear to carry a headboard. The locomotives are 37427 and 37430 [details on page 12]. Harlech is famous for the castle, which is to the right of this picture. The station opened on 10th October 1867 and is still open.

Date 16th May 1987. Gavin Morrison.

Penrhyndeudraeth is a small village on the coast with a population of just over 2,000. Part of the land has been reclaimed from the estuary of the Afon Glaslyn and Afon Dwryd. It will always be associated with the explosives industry, started in 1872 and developed by ICI when demand was great for World War 1 and 2. Otherwise the products were used in the slate quarries and mining industries. Over the years there were several fatal accidents and the factory closed in 1997. The quarry, where the explosives were stored, was cleared and is now a nature reserve. The SO 8.00 Pwllheli- Euston is seen crossing the road/rail bridge over the estuary. The station opened on the 2nd September 1867 and is still in use. [Details of class 37/4 No 37428 are on page 43].

Date 16th May 1985. Gavin Morrison. 59

Porthmadog has now become quite a railway centre with the recent reopening of the Welsh Highland Railway. It is the terminus of the Ffestiniog Railway and Network rail tracks pass through on their way to Pwllheli. Here, the up Snowdonian' is seen again entering the station headed by class 37/4s Nos 37427 and 37430 [details page 12].   *Date 16th May 1987. Gavin Morrison.*

This picture, taken from very near the position of the previous picture, shows how the station area has changed over the years. Class 4300 Mogul No 6392 is arriving with a train from Pwllheli. It was allocated to Machynlleth in October 1957, where it remained until withdrawn in September 1961. *Believed to be 1961. Railphotoprints.co.uk Alan H Bryant ARPS.*

Dukedog class 4-4-0 No 9012 was one of thirty built as late as 1936, by the GWR for the Cambrian Lines. No 9012 is recorded as being allocated to Machynlleth shed from nationalisation and probably before that. It was withdrawn on 15th June 1957 and is leaving Porthmadoc with a train to Barmouth.

Date 9th October 1951. Hugh Ballantyne.

The final picture on the Dovey Junction to Pwllheli line [54miles], shows the down 'Snowdonian', 7.40 SO Euston-Pwllheli headed by class 37/4s Nos 37430 and 37427[details page 12], arriving at Cricceth station, The loop and down platform were no longer in use. The station opened on the 2nd September 1867 and is still open. It is eight miles from the end of the line at Pwllheli.

Date 16 the May 1987. Gavin Morrison.

Two Buxton allocated class 37/5s are well away from their normal duties of hauling limestone trains in the Peak district. They are heading the 10.10 Aberysthwyth-Euston past Glandyfi, just to the west of Dovey Junction on the banks of the river Dovey. Both locomotives, Nos 37683 and 37682, are in the railfreight grey livery. [Locomotive details are on page 30.] *Date 24th. May 1988. Gavin Morrison.*

The down "Cambrian Coast Express" approaches Borth station It is now reduced to only 3 coaches after the Pwllheli portion was split off at Dovey Junction. No 7803 "Barcote Manor" is in the usual immaculate external condition as the trains regular engine at the time. Borth is only 7 miles from Aberysthwyth and is a popular holiday destination. The station opened on the 1st July 1863 and is still in use [Details of 7803 on page 28]   *Date 30th May 1964. Gavin Morrison.*

The up "Cambrian Coast Express," headed by BR standard 4MT No 75033 [details page 33], is passing Bow Street 4½ miles from Aberysthwyth and at the bottom of a dip with short 1 in 75 gradients either side. The station opened on the 23rd June 1864 and closed on 14th June 1965.The station and down platform can be seen on the left of the picture. *Date 11th February 1967. Gavin Morrison.*

On a crisp February morning, the up "Cambrian Coast Express" makes a spirited departure from Aberysthwyth. It is approaching Llanbadarn, headed by BR standard 4MT No 75048 [details on page 16]. Note the train is 7 coaches rather than 3. This was because the 4 coach Pwllheli portion had ceased running on the 3rd September 1966. The line was double track between Aberysthwyth and Llanbadarn but as can be seen, the down track was being dismantled.

Date 11th February 1967. Gavin Morrison.

Class 25s Nos. 25298 and 25254 leave Aberysthwyth on the SO 14.00 to Shrewsbury. [Locomotive details page 17]. The old steam shed can be seen on the left, which is now used by the Vale of Rheidol narrow gauge railway, whose track can be seen in the foreground, heading for Devil's Bridge 11¾ miles away and 700 feet higher. *Date 1st Seprember 1984. Gavin Morrison.*

There are few passengers boarding the up "Cambrian Coast Express" at Aberysthwyth station on a fine February morning, as a well cleaned [by enthusiasts] standard 4MT No 75048 prepares to leave for Shrewsbury. [Loco details page 16.]

Date 11th February 1967. Gavin Morrison. 69

Class 7800 4-6-0 No 7822 "Foxcote Manor" is in Aberysthwyth Station ready to depart with an evening train for Manchester. It was new in December 1950 and spent virtually all of its relatively short career [15 years] allocated to the Cambrian sheds. At the time of this picture it was at Oswestry shed, which was obviously very short of cleaners. After withdrawal on the 9th October 1965, it was eventually preserved and is now based at the Llangollen Railway.

Date 8th September 1962. Gavin Morrison.

After working the "Cambrian Coast Express" to Shrewabury and back during the day, No 7803 "Barcote Manor" is back on Aberysthwyth shed in the evening, a diagram of about 194 miles. [Loco details page 28.] *Date 30th May 1964. Gavin Morrison.*

The last up "Cambrian Coast Express," on the final day of steam on the Cambrian lines, prepares to leave Aberysthwyth with cleaned standard 4MT No 75033 [details page 33] Many enthusiasts tuned up to travel on the train and the local press arrived to record the occasion. The last down train left Shrewsbury behind a very dirty double chimney No 75006.   *Date 4th March 1967. Gavin Morrison.*